Love Like a Samaritan

Edwin L. Crozier

DeWard
for your journey

Love Like a Samaritan
© 2017 by DeWard Publishing Company, Ltd.
P.O. Box 6259, Chillicothe, Ohio 45601
800.300.9778
www.deward.com

Cover design by Eric Wallace.

Printed in the United States of America.

ISBN: 978-1-936341-93-1

CONTENTS

INTRODUCTION

I'd like to tell you a story.

A certain man was traveling from Jerusalem to Jericho when he fell among robbers and thieves. They beat him, stripped him, and left him half dead on the side of the road. By chance a priest was going down that road, and when he saw the man he passed by on the other side. Likewise a Levite, when he came down that same road and saw the man, he also passed by on the other side. But a Samaritan, as he travelled, came down that very same road. When he saw the man, he had compassion. He went to him and bound up his wounds, treating them with oil and wine. He set the injured man on his own animal and brought him to an inn and took care of him all that night. The next day he took out two days' wages and offered them to the innkeeper, saying, "Take care of him, and whatever more you spend I will repay you when I come back."

I know, I know, that isn't my story. I just copied it from Jesus. Most of us have heard this story of "The Good Samaritan."[1] It is one of the most famous stories ever told. And like any good story, when we dig beneath its surface, we discover manifold riches.

I need this story. I need to hear it again and again and again. Let me tell you another story.

---

[1] Found in *Luke* 10.30-35.

I had just completed a sermon series on the parable of the Good Samaritan. I had waxed eloquent about loving my neighbor and being zealous for good deeds. But I was in a hurry. I had spent my morning studying my Bible at a coffee shop in hopes of generating a conversation that would lead to me doing the good work of sharing the gospel and maybe saving a soul. I had found no such luck that day. Now it was time for lunch, and I was supposed to return home to have some family time. I was a little stressed because Indiana had been receiving a significant amount of snow. The roads were slick and slightly dangerous. I pulled up to the exit to turn to turn left out of the parking lot. A van two cars ahead of me started spinning out. "Great!" I thought. "I'm going to get stuck here." So I looked in my mirror, made an executive decision, and pulled over to the right lane to turn right and head home a different direction. Wouldn't you know it, the van driver stomped on his gas, started spinning wheels like crazy, slid across the road to the right, and ended up in front of the car that was now in front of me. "What!?" I already knew that, no matter which checkout line I picked at Wal-Mart, I would find the slow one, but did that curse have to hit me on the road too? I tried to merge left again, but the car that had been behind the van started to spin its wheels as well. "I'll never get home," I thought. But, not to be stopped, I dropped my Explorer into 4-wheel drive, squeezed between the two offending vehicles, and merrily made my way for a nice family lunch. About halfway home it hit me. A priest and a Levite were walking down that same road and they passed by on the other side. Oh snap!

Yes, I need to hear this story again and again and again. If I am not careful, I can get wrapped up in my world of neatly packaged religious works, think I'm being like Christ, but never let Him actually impact me where the rubber hits the road (or rather where the rubber is slipping and sliding all over the road). So I'm not writing this book to teach you anything. I'm writing this book to remind me of the neighbors all around me who are slipping and sliding on the road or, worse, who have been beaten, stripped, and left half dead. But if you can get something good out of this too, praise the Lord!

1

THE GOOD DEED

I'd like to tell you a story.

A certain man was traveling from Jerusalem to Jericho when he fell among robbers and thieves. They beat him, stripped him, and left him half dead on the side of the road. By chance a priest was going down that road, and when he saw the man he passed by on the other side. Likewise a Levite, when he came down that same road and saw the man, he also passed by on the other side. But a Samaritan, as he travelled, came down that very same road. When he saw the man, he had compassion. He went to him and bound up his wounds, treating them with oil and wine. He set the injured man on his own animal and brought him to an inn and took care of him all that night. The next day he took out two days' wages and gave them to the innkeeper, saying, "Take care of him, and whatever more you spend I will repay you when I come back."

Yeah, I know, you've heard this story before (unless you're one of those people who skips book introductions because you just want to get to the meat), but as I said, I need to hear the story again and again and again. After all, for many, this story is the touchstone of good deeds and loving our neighbor. Throughout this book, this story will be the outline for what it means to love our neighbors. However, from the very beginning, we do need to back up and recognize it isn't actually the touchstone. There is another story we need to remember, one which is the foundation for all our love and good deeds. It is a story that reminds us a good deed has been done for us that should change us.

But before we get to that story, let me tell you another story that was supposed to change people and let's notice how it impacted them. This story may disturb our modern sensitivities; however, I assure you it is a Bible story. In fact, God told this story to the Israelites. It is the story of a good deed. It is the story of The Good Deed for the nation of Israel. This story should have prompted good deeds from them. Here is the story.

God's Good Deed for Israel

An Amorite married a Hittite and together they produced a child. However, they hated the child. They abhorred it. So much did they despise this baby, they did not cut its cord, they did not clean it, they did not preserve it, they did not clothe it. They abandoned it. They left it covered in blood, languishing in its afterbirth, and tossed it into an open field. Egyptians passed by and did nothing. Philistines came by and did nothing. Canaanites came by and did nothing. The parents didn't even do anything. No one took pity. No one had compassion. No Samaritan came to the infant's aid.

But God came by, saw the baby laying in its filthy mess of blood, and said, "Live!" Because of God's love and compassion, the baby grew and flourished. But as it grew to maturity, it was naked and ashamed. Once again, no one was there to have compassion on this shameful sight. The Canaanites left her in abandonment. The Egyptians just took advantage of her nakedness. But God passed by again and covered her. He clothed her, adorning her with fine clothing, precious jewelry, and a beautiful crown. He gave her fine foods to eat. He took her as His bride. This woman, who had been brought up in naked shame, became His wife. She advanced to beauty and royalty. All those who had abandoned her and left her for dead recognized her beauty, and she had renown among the nations.

God told Israel this story in Ezekiel 16 to explain His good deed to them. When Abraham was called, he was the old husband of a barren wife. He was alone in a strange land. But God blessed Him with a son and grandsons. His great grandsons, Simeon and Levi, actually made his family anathema to the Canaanites by the slaughter of the Shechemites. They were in danger of being destroyed in the land. But God had made a covenant with them and brought them into Egypt to protect them. While there, they chased after other gods.[1] They were in a shameful state. But God brought them out of Egypt through plagues and with riches. Though they rebelled, He eventually brought them into the Promised Land, some of the most coveted land of the ancient world. The nation grew to great renown.

Several times a year the Israelites were reminded of this in the feasts they were prescribed. The Passover and Feast of Unleavened Bread reminded them of their hurried deliverance from Egypt on the night God passed over the Israelites but slew the firstborn of all the Egyptians. The Feast of Weeks (Pentecost) reminded them of their slavery in Egypt and the power of God that brought them into their own homeland, allowing them to farm for themselves. The Feast of Tabernacles (Booths) reminded them of the years in the wilderness as they lived in tents and God fed them and protected them.

---

[1] See Ezekiel 23.3.

What was all of this to accomplish? The Good Deed of God seeing them in the field in their blood and breathing life to them was supposed to prompt them to good deeds. In fact, in Exodus 20.2, as God introduced the 10 Commandments to Israel, He prefaced it with "I am the LORD your God, who brought you out of the land of Egypt, out of the house of slavery." The purpose for which God separated Israel from the nations was so they would be His own special possession devoted to serving Him (cf. Deuteronomy 26.18-19). But Israel did not pursue good deeds. The Good Deed of God did not prompt good deeds from them. Rather, they rebelled again and again and again.

Ezekiel 16 demonstrates they did not do good toward God or toward their fellow man. In Ezekiel 16.35-37, the Israelites pursued idolatry rather than serving the Lord. They worshiped the creature rather than the Creator. We learn that Israel went even farther than her younger sister Sodom. But notice the good they did not do according to Ezekiel 16.49: "Behold, this was the guilt of your sister Sodom: she and her daughters had pride, excess of food, and prosperous ease, but did not aid the poor and needy." Does this shock you like it does me? We know the abomination that was committed in Genesis 19, but despite our modern political controversies and use of Sodom's story, God's great concern in this verse was the fact that His Good Deed for them didn't prompt them to share good deeds with others. For all of Israel's existence as a nation, they were to look back at God's Good Deed in delivering them from Egyptian slavery to the Promised Land as the motivation and standard by which they lived. But they didn't. They took pride in all that God had given them as if it were their own making and turned from God (cf. Ezekiel 16.15ff). They even used God's gifts as a means to commit spiritual adultery. God's Good Deed no longer kept them safe because they no longer valued God's Good Deed.

God's Good Deed for Us

I'd like to tell you another story. I did make this one up... kind of.

A man was walking home one day, minding his own business, when he was accosted by a robber who beat him, stripped him, maimed him, and left him lame and half-dead. The man tried to crawl to the nearest emergency room for help, but every time he thought he was going to get away, the robber would appear and beat him some more, dragging him back. By chance, a woman came down the road, but before she could help, the robber attacked her as well, leaving her half dead, unable to help. A little later, a church-attender came down that very road. But when he saw the beaten pair, he was certain this could only happen to people who did not follow God's law as well as he did. Afraid the robber might still be lurking by, he crossed to the other side of the street to protect himself. Just when the church-attender thought he had escaped danger by his own strength, the robber shot him from his dark hiding place.

A little later, a lowly Jew walked that way. He saw the couple and stooped to help. The robber, seeing his vulnerability, attacked the Jewish man. He beat him, called him names, mocked him, but steadily the Jewish man worked to carry the people to safety, not succumbing to the robber's attacks. Though he stumbled beneath the beating he received, he protected the people through these continuing attacks. Though his own lifeblood was leaving him, he continued to bear these half-dead people. He was gasping for breath as he faced the continuing onslaught of the attack. He brought them to the emergency room and delivered them into the care of the doctor. With his dying breath, he gave the doctor payment to heal the wounds of the ones he had brought. He died so they could live.

Do I even need to explain this parable? It tells the story of The Good Deed. It is our story. We, like Paul in Romans 7.7-10, were walking the path of our life. But sin and Satan, using the law of God, attacked us, destroyed us, and dominated us. As Paul said in Romans 7.21-23, we determined to do right and save ourselves, but sin and Satan were close at hand, beating us and dragging us back into our sinfulness. No doubt some believe they can save themselves from this attack. They are the strong ones. They are the "Older Brothers," if you will (see another great Bible story in Luke 15.25-32). Because of their self-righteousness, they have no compassion but treat others with contempt (see Luke 18.9). They provide no help, and in the end they die themselves without the aid of any to save them.

But we have a Savior. We have a Savior who did not wait until we fixed ourselves, but offered Himself in our place while we were still sinners, weak, and ungodly (Romans 5.6-8). To truly understand The Good Deed, consider Philippians 2.5-8. Jesus, God the Son, sacrificed the glories of heaven. To come down to this world, He let go of the appearance and form of deity that demands a worship response from any who come into His presence. Not only that, but He didn't enter this world as royalty. He entered this world as a poor carpenter's son in an enslaved nation. He entered under the cloud of the suspicion of immorality because everyone knew His mother became pregnant before she was married. He grew up in a town that everyone despised—the armpit of the enslaved nation, if you will. Though He did amazing things and amassed multitudes of followers, in the end the majority of His followers rejected Him and betrayed Him, demanding His death. Even those who didn't betray Him abandoned Him. They didn't understand. But a couple of them watched as Jesus was beaten, scourged, crowned with thorns, and tormented by men whom He could have squashed like bugs. Then He was nailed to a cross. He was taunted and ridiculed. The people who saw Him thought He was being punished by God. But as Isaiah promised, "He was wounded for our transgressions, he was crushed for our iniquities; upon him was the chastisement that brought us peace, and with his stripes we are healed" (Isaiah 53.5). In those moments, I believe He was separated from the Father. Because of our sins, the Father looked away and the divine fellowship Jesus enjoyed was severed. Can you imagine the spiritual agony that accompanied the physical?

For whom did Jesus do this? Did He do it for people who deserved it? Did He do it for people who could pay Him back? Did He do it for people to whom He was obligated? No. He did it for sinners who had spit in His face. He did it for ungodly people who had rejected Him. He did it for weak people who had been complicit with His enemy. He did it for you. He did it for me.

Why did He do it? Because like the Good Samaritan, He simply had compassion on us. He bestows mercy on us. Why? Because, as John 3.16 says, He loves us.

Please understand what this is. This is The Good Deed. This is the Good Samaritan times infinity. This is the epitome of good deeds. It is the motivation for our good deeds. It is the standard by which our good deeds will be judged. It is the guide for our good deeds. When we consider how we should respond to God, we should see Jesus on the cross for us. When we consider how we should treat our brothers and sisters in Christ, we should see Jesus on the cross for us. When we consider how we should treat those who are still in the world, we should see Jesus on the cross for them. When Satan tempts us to withhold good from those around us, we should see Satan tempting Jesus to abandon the cross and leave us in our sins and how in reality we deserve abandonment. And we should see Jesus telling Satan to get behind Him. Everything else we ever learn about loving like a Samaritan comes right back to this, the supreme, the epitome, the ultimate, The Good Deed. We will be challenged, but remember, Jesus has not asked anything of us He hasn't already done for us.

2

WHO DO YOU LOVE?

I'd like to tell you a story.

A certain man was traveling from Jerusalem to Jericho when he fell among robbers and thieves. They beat him, stripped him, and left him half dead on the side of the road. By chance a priest was going down that road, and when he saw the man he passed by on the other side. Likewise a Levite, when he came down that same road and saw the man, he also passed by on the other side. But a Samaritan, as he travelled, came down that very same road. When he saw the man, he had compassion. He went to him and bound up his wounds, treating them with oil and wine. He set the injured man on his own animal and brought him to an inn and took care of him all that night. The next day he took out two days' wages and gave them to the innkeeper, saying, "Take care of him, and whatever more you spend, I will repay you when I come back."

But Jesus didn't tell this story in a vacuum. So let's back up and see the whole story. A lawyer stood up to put Jesus to the test, asking, "Teacher, what shall I do to inherit eternal life?" Jesus said to him, "What is written in the Law? How do you read it?" And the lawyer answered, "You shall love the Lord your God with all your heart and with all your soul and with all your strength and with all your mind, and your neighbor as yourself." And Jesus responded, "You have answered correctly; do this, and you will live." But the lawyer, desiring to justify himself, said to Jesus, "And who is my neighbor?" Then Jesus told the story of the beaten Jew and the benevolent Samaritan. Do you see the question the Samaritan's story answers? Who is my neighbor? Jesus and the lawyer both agreed, if the lawyer wanted eternal life he must love God and his neighbor. But the lawyer wasn't finished. This wasn't a clear enough answer. He needed better lines drawn. So he asked, "Who is my neighbor?" Think about the question behind this question. The lawyer wants to know, "Who do I have to love to secure eternal life?"

Isn't this the same question we ask even after hearing the story of the benevolent Samaritan? Okay, I'm supposed to love my neighbor, but who is that? Who do I have to love?

A Lawyer Kind of Answer

To really grasp how amazing this story is, let's consider what the lawyer was actually looking for. What kind of answer did he expect Jesus to give or, rather, what kind of answer did he want Jesus to give him.

Lawyers were teachers of the Law who worked hard to figure out the jots and tittles of legal application. They knew the Law well. They had figured out the patterns. They had figured out the applications. They knew the loopholes. They knew the limitations. They knew how far you could go and how far you had to go. They knew what you had to do to fulfill commands. They figured things out like how many times you were really allowed to strike someone when legally punishing them, how far you could actually walk on a Sabbath's day journey, and which spices you had to tithe. They liked lines and limitations.

When this lawyer said, "Who is my neighbor?" this is the kind of question he was asking. What's the limitation on this? "Sure, Jesus, I know I'm supposed to love my neighbor. But who does that really mean? What is the limitation? Let's be reasonable. God couldn't mean I have to love everyone, so who do I actually have to love?" I hope we grasp this. The lawyer's question was one we hear asked very often and one we often ask ourselves. The question was "Do I have to...?" The lawyer might as well have been pointing his finger at different people and asking, "Do I have to love that guy?" In fact, he was actually asking, "Surely I don't have to love everyone to get eternal life. Who can I get away with not loving?"

The lawyer was looking for Jesus to provide acceptable limits that drew a circle around those he actually had to love to make this command easier. He expected an answer listing qualifications—must be a Jew, must live in the Promised Land, must be part of your own tribe, must be within a Sabbath's day journey of your home, etc. The lawyer's question wasn't really about who he had to love. It was really about who he could get away with not loving. And isn't that the basis of all our "do I have to" questions?

A Truly Shocking Story

One of the things I missed for a long time is the cultural setting behind this story. Jesus does a masterful job setting it up. Remember, the story begins by saying the lawyer stood up to put Jesus to the test. He was trying to entrap Jesus in His words. We don't know the exact nature of this trap, but in some way he wanted Jesus to fail in His words and lose face before the crowds. But Jesus turns the tables and springs a huge trap on the lawyer.

For a long time I have been aware that the Jews and the Samaritans didn't like each other. The Samaritans descended from the non-Jews who had come into Israel when Assyria took the northern kingdom captive. God sent lions among those inhabitants who were not worshiping Him in His land. So the Assyrians sent Levites to teach them how to worship God. However, they didn't devote themselves completely to God; they simply added Him to their group of gods (cf. 2 Kings 17). The Jews hated those imitators. They despised their half-religion and half-devotion. They abhorred the fact that they didn't worship in Jerusalem. And because the Jews rightly refused to allow the half-religion of the Samaritans to be part of their worship, the Samaritans hated the Jews with perhaps equal vehemence.

However, there is another aspect to this story that I missed for a long time. Among the Jews, there were multiple sects or groups that adhered to different philosophies. Two of the most well-known were the Sadducees and the Pharisees. Pharisees were semi-separatists who wanted to make a huge distinction between Jews and everyone else by keeping the Law as strictly as possible. They did believe in the resurrection. They believed they would gain eternal life because of their strict adherence to the Law of Moses. Most lawyers and scribes were Pharisees. This lawyer who is concerned about inheriting eternal life is almost certainly a Pharisee.

The Sadducees on the other hand were materialists who didn't believe in the resurrection (cf. Luke 20.27; Acts 23.8). Thus, Sadducees wouldn't be very worried about inheriting eternal life. The two groups were rivals. They didn't really like each other. Pharisees thought the Sadducees were materialistic opportunists who weren't really concerned with keeping God's people separate from the Romans and other Gentiles. The Sadducees saw the Pharisees as extremists who were going to keep

Israel in trouble with Rome and mess up their material opportunities in the Empire. Here is the kicker. Many priests and Levites were Sadducees.[1]

Understanding that, do you see what Jesus did with this story? He was answering a Pharisee or at least someone who had leanings toward the Pharisees. He told the story about a priest and a Levite, men who would likely have been Sadducees and how they passed by a man in need. I can almost see the lawyer salivating. Jesus was slapping the lawyer's religious rivals. As Jesus started to talk about the third man walking past the Jew, who do you think the lawyer expected to be the hero? Jesus had just shown how those materialistic, unspiritual Sadducees responded. Surely He was going to bring up a good, law-abiding Pharisee. Instead, He introduced someone even worse than the Sadducees. He brought in a Samaritan.

To really grasp how shocking this story was to the lawyer, imagine Jesus was standing with you and a group of your friends and He told a similar story. He might tell it like this:

A man was driving down the road when he was carjacked by hoods that beat him, robbed him, stripped him. They stole his car and left him for dead on the side of the road. By chance one of those Christians who thinks God created the world through the big bang and evolution drove down that same road. When he saw the injured man, he gunned his engines and sped by. Likewise, one of those Christians who questions if Genesis 1-12 is literal passed that way. When he saw the man, he didn't even slow down, but sped by. But after a time an Atheist came by, picked up the man, washed the man with his own bottled water, ripped

---

[1] Consider Acts 5.17. I certainly don't want to paint with too broad of a brush. Clearly, someone like Zechariah, father of John the Baptizer, was a priest who believed in the spiritual realm (Luke 1.5-25). However, it appears many priests and Levites did walk with the Sadducees.

up his own shirt to wrap the man's wounds, and set his bloody and grime-covered body on his leather seats. He carried the man to a nearby hospital. Once he carried the man inside, he gave the hospital his own financial information so they could charge him instead of the injured man.

Would you be shocked?

This was so shocking to the lawyer that when Jesus asked him who proved to be the neighbor to the beaten man, the lawyer couldn't even say, "The Samaritan." I hope I'm not making too much of this as one friend of mine says I do. But it almost seems as if he choked on that and instead said, "The one who showed him mercy." What would we have said if Jesus had just told a story showing us up by using an Atheist as the hero?

A Better Question

When Jesus finished His story, He turned to the lawyer and sprung His trap with a question. But have you ever noticed how odd His question is? He didn't ask who was the Levite's neighbor, who was the priest's neighbor, or who was the Samaritan's neighbor. He didn't actually ask simply who was the beaten Jew's neighbor. The English Standard provides a more challenging translation when it shows Jesus asking, "Who proved to be a neighbor to the man who fell among the robbers?" I'm not a Greek expert, but this does seem to accurately express Jesus's point. Who proved to be a neighbor? Who showed himself to be a neighbor? As *Young's Literal Translation* puts it, who became this man's neighbor? Why would Jesus ask this in such an odd way?

Jesus was highlighting that the lawyer had asked the wrong question. The lawyer asked, "Who is my neighbor?" He essentially asked, "Who do I have to love?" "Who meets the qualifications of being my neighbor so that I am obligated to love him?" Or, as we more accurately noted, "Who can I get away with not loving?" Jesus deftly explained that those were bad questions. The right question is not who qualifies as my neighbor. The right question is how do I qualify as a neighbor? Rather than asking who do I have to love, I need to ask, "How do I prove myself to be someone who loves?"

The lawyer was asking for lines and limitations, but Jesus didn't give any. In fact, if you're like me, when you get done with this story you are left thinking, "Well, that doesn't help me at all. Okay, I'm supposed to go and do likewise, but for whom? I mean when I see a broken down car, do I have to stop? When a beggar is at the side of the road, do I have to give him something? How much do I have to give him? Do I have to help non-Christians? Who do I have to love?" Jesus actually didn't answer those questions for us. At least not directly. He doesn't draw the lines that let us off the hook. He challenges us with His shocking story. He challenges us with His pointed question. He refuses to spoon feed us and make it easy.

But He does make it very clear that loving my neighbor, as with all spiritual maturity, is about asking good questions, asking the right question. And the right question is not "Who is my neighbor?" The better question is "How do I prove to be a neighbor?"

So Who Is My Neighbor?

Now that you've considered Jesus's odd question for a moment, let's take another look at it and how He really is answering the lawyer's question. The lawyer's question is "Who is my neighbor?" Jesus's better question is "Who proved to be the beaten man's neighbor?"

Put yourself in this lawyer's shoes. In this story, with whom would he have most closely identified? He was no Levite or priest. He didn't want to be. They were likely Sadducees who didn't believe in eternal life. He wanted to know how to gain eternal life, and they wouldn't care about that. He was no robber. That was clearly against the Law. He would never do anything as rebellious as stealing from someone. He wouldn't beat anyone and leave them half dead. He certainly didn't identify with the Samaritan, that mixed-religion, pagan Jewish wannabe. With whom would he have most closely identified? The beaten man.

Do you see now the masterful stroke Jesus played here? The lawyer asked, "Who is my neighbor?" He essentially asked, "Who qualifies to be someone I have to love?" Jesus tells a story that essentially responds, "I don't know, lawyer. Who would you want to be your neighbor if you were lying half-dead on the side of the road? Would you refuse a Samaritan's help if you were the one beaten and dying? Then why would you refuse to help him if he were the one beaten?"

And this is the problem for us. None of us ever asks, "Who should show me mercy?" We think anyone and everyone should show us mercy and compassion. If we were beaten, dying, hungry, thirsty, naked, in need, we wouldn't hand someone an application that they had to fill out in triplicate to prove they really were our neighbor and therefore were obligated to help us. But do we ask, "Who do I have to love? Who is my neighbor?" Do we put people through a background check and neighbor assessment test before we will show them mercy? Jesus responds, "Your neighbor is anyone you would want to help you if they passed by when roles were reversed."

My Problem

This sums up my problem and the reason I need to hear this story again and again and again. Too often I ask the wrong question. Too often I want the limits, the rules, the regulations. Who do I really have to love? To whom do I really have to show mercy and compassion? I should quit asking who my neighbors are and instead ask how I can prove to be a better neighbor. How can I be a better neighbor to those who cross my path, whether it is a family member, a co-worker, a person in my neighborhood, a school-mate, a brother or sister in Christ, a stranded driver, a homeless man on the street, or whoever else?

Our story ends with Jesus insisting, "You go, and do likewise." That leaves us with this question. Who do you love?

3

A NEXT LEVEL KIND OF LOVE

I'd like to tell you a story.

A certain man was traveling from Jerusalem to Jericho when he fell among robbers and thieves. They beat him, stripped him, and left him half dead on the side of the road. By chance a priest was going down that road and when he saw the man, he passed by on the other side. Likewise a Levite, when he came down that same road and saw the man, he also passed by on the other side. But a Samaritan, as he travelled, came down that very same road. When he saw the man, he had compassion. He went to him and bound up his wounds, treating them with oil and wine. He set the injured man on his own animal and brought him to an inn and took care of him all that night. The next day he took out two days' wages and gave them to the innkeeper, saying, "Take care of him, and whatever more you spend, I will repay you when I come back."

As we learned in the previous chapter, Jesus didn't tell this story in a vacuum. He told it when a lawyer asked him what he needed to do to inherit eternal life. He turned the question back on the lawyer asking him what he read in the Law. The man said to love God and love your neighbor as yourself. Jesus agreed, but the lawyer wasn't happy with that answer. He wanted better lines drawn. So he asked, "Who is my neighbor?" Then Jesus told this story.

But we recognize that Jesus was actually telling the lawyer to ask a better question. "How do I prove to be a neighbor?" We may be tempted to think Jesus left us on our own when it comes to answering this question. But He didn't. His story itself is a masterful look at being a good neighbor. Let me show you how Jesus accomplished this.

The Law on Loving Your Neighbor

When the lawyer said he believed the Law taught he had to love his neighbor as himself to inherit eternal life, he wasn't just pulling some idea out of thin air. He wasn't summarizing all the law into two pithy statements he had developed from his own study. He was quoting Leviticus 19.18: "You shall not take vengeance or bear a grudge against the sons of your own people, but you shall love your neighbor as yourself: I am the Lord."

The context of this quote is fascinating.

When you reap the harvest of your land, you shall not reap your field right up to its edge, neither shall you gather the gleanings after your harvest. And you shall not strip your vineyard bare, neither shall you gather the fallen grapes of your vineyard. You shall leave them for the poor and for the sojourner: I am the LORD your God.

You shall not steal; you shall not deal falsely; you shall not lie to one another. You shall not swear by my name falsely, and so profane the name of your God: I am the LORD

You shall not oppress your neighbor or rob him. The wages of a hired servant shall not remain with you all night until the morning. You shall not curse the deaf or put a stumbling block before the blind, but you shall fear your God: I am the LORD.

You shall do no injustice in court. You shall not be partial to the poor or defer to the great, but in righteousness shall you judge your neighbor. You shall not go around as a slanderer among your people, and you shall not stand up against the life of your neighbor: I am the LORD.

You shall not hate your brother in your heart, but you shall reason frankly with your neighbor, lest you incur sin because of him. You shall not take vengeance or bear a grudge against the sons of your own people, but you shall love your neighbor: I am the LORD (Leviticus 19.9-18).

When I read this law on loving our neighbors, I discovered that the story of the benevolent Samaritan is far deeper and more profound than I had ever imagined. Jesus's masterfully told story actually ties back to this passage about loving your neighbor. As we compare Jesus's story to this section of the Law, we are reminded again and again of how to prove ourselves someone's neighbor.

Loving at the Next Level

The lawyer, of course, would want to take Leviticus 19.9-18 and parse every word, analyze every grammatical structure, and weed out every rule and requirement. His hope was to dot the Is and cross the Ts so he could prove he had loved acceptably and deserved eternal life. But Jesus's story actually blows right past these legal requirements and says we prove we are good neighbors when we move past the legal stipulations in order to love at the next level. Walk through the law on loving our neighbor and see how Jesus's story reflects back to it.

Whose Stuff Is It Anyway?

The first legal requirement for the Jews to love their neighbors in Leviticus 19.9-10 was don't glean all the way to the edges of their fields but leave some behind for the poor and the foreigner. They were not to hoard their goods but set aside part of it for others less blessed. The lawyer, knowing this law, would leave some grapes and olives in his fields and vineyards. But then he had fulfilled the Law. What more would he possibly have to do? The Law didn't say anything about using some of his oil and wine to serve the downtrodden. The lawyer would find the line. The line was drawn back at the vineyard and olive grove.

However, when the Samaritan came upon the beaten Jew, he used his own oil and wine to help treat the man's wounds. He didn't draw the line back at his vineyard. He didn't meet some legal line of love and then hoard the rest of his own blessings. He sacrificed his oil and wine for someone less blessed. The Samaritan didn't dicker about the lines. He took the Law to its next level.

The purpose of this legal stipulation was to teach God's people to help others in need by sacrificing one's own resources for those others, not provide a hoop to jump through so lawyers could claim eternal life because they measured up.

Loving our neighbor means recognizing God has blessed us to be a blessing to others. Do we set aside some of our blessings to be used for those less blessed, or do we spend all we have and then borrow so we can't devote anything we have to help others? More than that, after we have set aside some for others, do we ever find ourselves cutting into what is left over because someone else needs it? The lawyer knew the law about loving his neighbor, but the Samaritan took it to the next level.

But I'm Very Religious

God's legal stipulation about not swearing by God's name falsely in Leviticus 19.12 doesn't seem at first glance to apply to loving our neighbor. It almost seems out of place. We're talking about loving our neighbor, not about loving God. But Jesus's story about a Levite and a priest connects the two loves.

How often do you think the Levite and the priest swore by God's name? How often did they call on God's name? How often did they declare they were God's people? They wore God's name like a badge. I don't know exactly what excuse the priest and Levite offered, but I've heard several point out that they could have used their service to God as an excuse. If they had helped the man and he had died while they were carrying him, they would have become unclean before God. If they were on their way to perform duties at the temple, they wouldn't have been able to. How bad would that have been?

Whatever their actual excuse, when they saw this dying man, they left him to die. Were they not wearing God's name falsely? When they called on God to be a witness to their dedication and devotion to Him, didn't their passing by this dying man show that God would have to witness against them? The Jewish lawyer would have claimed that any time a Samaritan swore by God, he did so falsely because he wasn't worshiping God properly. In fact, the lawyer might pass by the beaten man and use his strict religious practice as justification. "I may not have helped the beaten man, but I keep God's Law about worshiping Him better than you do." The Samaritan on the other hand recognized that swearing by God wasn't just about going to the temple but about how we act from day to day.

This reminds me of a story I once read but unfortunately can't remember which book I read it in. A young teenage lady who claimed to be a Christian, when asked out on a date by a young man, loudly and proudly proclaimed that she didn't date non-Christians, much to the public embarrassment of the young man who had worked up the nerve to ask her out. Later that day, on a pop quiz, this same young lady accepted a cheat sheet from a friend to help with the test. Someone noticed and also proclaimed: "I guess the girl who can't date a non-Christian can accept a cheat-sheet from one." And this hits me where it hurts (remember that poor guy in his van who couldn't get out of the parking lot in our introduction?) How easy it is to think my religious observances and work makes up for avoiding simple neighbor love.

It is amazing that Jesus would use a person who didn't love God properly to teach a lesson on loving like God properly. The point is not, of course, that if we love our neighbor it doesn't matter how we worship. The point is it doesn't matter how we worship if we don't love our neighbor. Do we love like lawyers? Do we bypass people in need, not helping, and justify our lack of love because we follow the pattern better than everyone else? Or do we love like the Samaritan. The lawyer knew the legal requirement for loving his neighbor, but the Samaritan took it to the next level.

Hanging Out at the Line

In Leviticus 19.11, 13, God told the Jews not to steal from or rob their neighbor. The lawyer would proudly profess he had never robbed anyone. The passing priest and Levite might defend themselves by pointing out that they didn't actually rob the man or oppress him. The lawyer had a great legal defense to prove he loved people enough. He had always lived by this statement. There's the line, and he had never crossed it.

But the Samaritan took this to the next level. The Samaritan recognized that passing by the beaten man was essentially the same thing as beating him. He may not have hit the man, but if he refused to help him recover, he might as well have been part of the robbers' band. He may not have stolen from the man, but if he didn't use his own resources to help the man who no longer had any resources of his own, he might as well have stolen from him.

The lawyer would insist the person's plight was not his fault. He would parse and proclaim the lines found in Leviticus 19.11, 13. The Samaritan didn't worry about blame; he just loved. The lawyer knew the legal requirement for loving his neighbor, but the Samaritan refused to hang out at the lines. He took his love to the next level.

The Wages of Love

In Leviticus 19.13, God told the Jews not to withhold wages from an employee. That, of course, has some application all on its own for Christians who employ or contract work from others. But the lawyer would proudly declare he had always loved his neighbor because he always paid what he owed people. If you worked for a day for the lawyer, he paid you the denarius he owed you.

However, the Samaritan gave two denarii, or two days' wages, to the innkeeper on behalf of this beaten man with the promise of more. The beaten man had never done a day's work for the Samaritan, but the Samaritan sacrificed two days' wages plus more for this man. He didn't owe this man anything, but how could he withhold this good? In fact, in I John 3.16-18, the apostle John drives this same point home. We don't just give to those we owe. When we see someone in need and we have the ability to help, we give to them as well.

The lawyer knew the legal stipulation to pay what he owed. But the Samaritan took his love to the next level.

Unseen Love

In Leviticus 19.14, God said not to curse the deaf or put a stumbling block before the blind, but rather fear God. The point is that the Jews were not to take advantage of those who couldn't do anything to stop them. Someone might curse a deaf person because the deaf will not hear and the one cursing can get away with it. Someone might put a stumbling block before a blind person because the blind will not see them and the one casting the stumbling block can get away with it. Most people simply fear the ones they are cursing or casting a stumbling block in front of. But if those ones are deaf and blind, the ones cursing and casting may think they have nothing to fear. The Jews, however, were to fear God who hears and sees all and will call them into account.

Of course, the lawyer would again point out that he hadn't beaten the man. He hadn't left the man for dead, so he had no reason to fear God. He was good. But the Samaritan didn't trust in the fact that he hadn't cursed the man or caused him to stumble. He knew ignoring a man who was suffering from someone else's curse and stumbling block was tantamount to being the curser.

I can imagine the Levite and the priest both felt they had nothing to fear. After all, the beaten man was dying. He would never let anyone know what they had done. Additionally, why help a man who couldn't do anything in return? But the Samaritan understood we shouldn't love our neighbor just to keep from upsetting him or in order to gain a reward. We should love our neighbor because we love God.

The lawyer may have known the law on loving his neighbor, but the Samaritan took his love to the next level.

Love on Trial

God told the Jews not to do injustice in court in Leviticus 19.15-16. He went on to say they were not to be partial either to the poor or the rich. Further, they weren't to slander others and stand up against their lives. The point was that they should not pervert justice and bear a false witness against anyone for any reason. They were not to receive bribes to slander a neighbor in court so that he would be judged and possibly executed. Notice how God says it: "you shall not stand up against the life [blood] of your neighbor."

The lawyer would likely say the beaten Jew was not standing on trial in a court. This doesn't seem to apply to their situation. However, there is a real sense in which the beaten man is very much on trial. Consider this. How often do we put those who are less blessed on trial before we will aid them? How often do we become judge and jury over why they got into the mess they are in before we will help them? Again, we don't know why the Levite and priest passed by, but another excuse they might have offered is that this must have been God's judgment against the man. Surely this wouldn't have happened to him if he had been right with God like they were. Who were they to intervene when God had brought this calamity upon him? If such was their thinking (and all too often it is ours), then they were putting the man on trial, and they were standing up against his life in their own kangaroo court of law.

The Samaritan thought differently. Who was he to stand up against the life of this man he didn't even know? He would be violating love if he testified falsely against this man in court; how much more if he judged him unworthy of help and good deeds in his own personal court?

The lawyer knew the rule on loving his neighbor, but the Samaritan took it to the next level.

Unbegrudging Love

As God wrapped up His legal requirements for loving neighbors, He told the Jews they were not to take vengeance or bear a grudge against the sons of their own people but should love their neighbor as themselves. If the lawyer was looking for a line on who was his neighbor, who he really had to love, this would have been the place to go. Surely the lawyer's neighbor was only a "son of your own people." It was only against the Jews that the lawyer had to avoid holding grudges.

But who proved to be the man's neighbor in Jesus's story? A man against whom the Jews bore a grudge and wanted to take vengeance. Samaritans were mistreated and reviled by the Jews, and the feeling was pretty mutual. There was a whole lot of grudge-bearing and vengeance that went on between them. But the Samaritan didn't even hesitate to think about that. He simply saw a man in need and helped him. If tables were turned, the lawyer would probably insist the Samaritan was not a son of his own people and therefore didn't get love from him. The Samaritan simply saw a creation of God in need and showed him mercy and compassion. He did not worry about lineage, value, or worth. He simply saw the need and met it. The Samaritan didn't kick the man and claim, "You deserve it, you Jewish bum." He didn't revel because the robbers got a Jew instead of a Samaritan. He didn't rejoice that another Jewish man would die. He helped the man.

How do we react when the person in need is someone we have something against? How do we react when it is someone who has hurt us? How do we react when it is someone who doesn't live like we do? The lawyer knew the legal stipulation about loving his neighbor, a son of his own people. But the Samaritan took his love to the next level.

A Lawyer's Love Versus a Samaritan's Love

As we wrap up this chapter, I want to sum up this next-level kind of love. I need to put myself to the test. How about you? What kind of love do we have? Do we live as good neighbors? Do we love like a lawyer or like this Samaritan? Consider some contrasts, and ask which side of this line you fall on.

A Lawyer's Love	The Samaritan's Love
Comes from obligation	Comes from mercy and compassion
Aims to gain blessing	Aims to share blessing
Pays back	Gives freely
Seeks to preserve its goods	Sacrifices
Is an event	Is a process
Refrains from harm	Actively helps
Is given to those they judge worthy	Is given to those who need it
Is for friends	Is for even enemies
Believes loving God makes up for not loving its neighbors	Knows really loving God is really loving its neighbors
Looks for lines and limitations	Is a next-level kind of love

A Look in the Mirror

I need to spend some time looking in the mirror. I need to spend some time asking whether or not I'm proving to be anyone's neighbor. Do I love like the lawyer or like the Samaritan? I've had to realize I am all too often like the lawyer. Amazingly enough, even after reading the story of the beaten Jew and the benevolent Samaritan, I usually end up with questions like, "Yeah, but I can't do that for everyone, so who do I really have to do that for? Do I have to stop for every stalled car? Do I have to give something to every begging bum? Do I have to donate to every possible charity? I can't do all of that. Surely God doesn't expect that of me." I spend a lot of my time asking, "Do I have to? What happens if I don't? Will I lose eternal life if I don't?" The fact is nobody can do everything. But what amazes me is Jesus doesn't provide limits. He doesn't hand me my copouts to avoid opportunities to love. He just challenges me. He tells me a story that places loving my neighbor on a practically unattainable level and then says, "You go and do likewise."

Perhaps the real problem is that all too often I am asking this question from the same motivation the lawyer was. This whole thing started with, "Teacher, what shall I do to inherit eternal life?" I continue to think I'm trying to jump through hoops and requirements to get to heaven. The problem is, if that is the journey I'm going to try to take to eternal life, it ain't going to happen. I can't possibly love that thoroughly, that completely, that universally. I don't have the resources, the time, the strength. As long as I'm trying to earn God's blessing of eternal life by jumping through hoops of love, I'll only despair. Instead, I need to recognize that God loved me first and let my love flow from that. I don't love in order to get life; I love because God has given me life. If I'm going to be like the Samaritan, I won't try to figure out who I have to love to get to heaven. Rather, I pass along the love God has given me when I can, where I can, and to whomever I can. I have to resist softening this chapter by asking if I actually have to do something. Rather, I must learn to simply pursue life asking how I can love the person I'm with the way God has loved me.

How about you?

4

SEEKING TO JUSTIFY HIMSELF

I'd like to tell you a story.

A certain man was traveling from Jerusalem to Jericho when he fell among robbers and thieves. They beat him, stripped him, and left him half dead on the side of the road. By chance a priest was going down that road and when he saw the man, he passed by on the other side. Likewise a Levite, when he came down that same road and saw the man, he also passed by on the other side. But a Samaritan, as he travelled, came down that very same road. When he saw the man, he had compassion. He went to him and bound up his wounds, treating them with oil and wine. He set the injured man on his own animal and brought him to an inn and took care of him all that night. The next day he took out two days' wages and gave them to the innkeeper, saying, "Take care of him, and whatever more you spend, I will repay you when I come back."

Perhaps this story is already getting old to you. However, instead, I hope it is impacting you on deeper and more profound levels. Don't forget Jesus ended the whole story with, "You, go, and do likewise." We need to be reminded of this story again and again.

We've already learned it wasn't told in a vacuum. This was Jesus's answer to a question: "Who is my neighbor?" (Luke

10.29). But why did the lawyer even ask this question? Was his question genuine? Was he concerned about all those neighbors out there who needed love? Did he know of a lot of people who were not loving their neighbors and he wanted Jesus to help them out? Was he trying to get an answer to a question he had struggled with all his life? Was he trying to get a leg up in an ongoing debate on this issue of neighbors? Why did he ask this question?

Why Did the Lawyer Ask?

Sadly, the lawyer was not asking a genuine question. Two statements in the larger context of Jesus's story drive this home.

First, notice Luke 10.25—"And behold, a lawyer stood up to put him to the test…" The text does not say, "A lawyer stood up to gain insight…" It doesn't say, "A lawyer stood up to understand God's will…" It doesn't say, "A lawyer stood up to get some help…" The lawyer was trying to lay a trap for Jesus. I don't fully understand how he hoped to trip Jesus up. Probably, the lawyer believed that almost any answer to this question could be disputed. This is one of those "give him enough rope and he'll hang himself" questions. The lawyer, probably having too much faith in his own knowledge of the Law, was certain Jesus would either say too much or not enough. In either case, he could accuse Jesus of disregarding God's Law. But the point we need to understand is the lawyer wasn't asking out of genuineness; he was asking in order to make Jesus look bad.

Second, notice Luke 10.29—"But he, desiring to justify himself, said to Jesus, 'And who is my neighbor?'" The text does not say, "But he, seeking to understand better…" It doesn't say, "But he, wanting to know more…" It doesn't say, "But he, hoping to gain deeper insight…" He was trying to justify himself.

Whatever kind of trap the lawyer had hoped to spring on Jesus was turned on him. He had asked a question, "What shall I do to inherit eternal life?" And then he immediately demonstrated that he already knew the answer. Now he looked foolish. In fact, he looked disingenuous. Everyone listening was figuring out that the lawyer wasn't actually trying to have a good discussion about eternal life; he was just trying to trap Jesus. (Actually, this sounds like a lot of religious discussions I read on Facebook.) So, he needed to salvage the situation. He needed to say something that would make it look like he really needed a good answer to help him on his walk to eternal life. So he asked about the neighbor. But again, he wasn't genuinely asking; he was simply trying to make himself look good.

Put that together and we conclude that the Lawyer wasn't actually trying to learn anything. He wanted to do two things. 1) Make Jesus look bad. 2) Make himself look good. Not a great starting point.

Justifying Himself

What does Luke mean when he records that the lawyer was trying to justify himself? Justifying is what we do when our conscience has been pricked. Here's how it works. You do something you know you shouldn't or perhaps don't do something you know you should. Your conscience starts to bother you. You have a choice. You either confess, repent, and come back in line with what you know is right or start to justify yourself.

For example: "I wasn't lusting; I was admiring beauty." "I didn't lie; I just withheld information that I didn't have to tell you." "I wasn't gossiping; I was just asking for your prayers on someone else's behalf because of a problem I know they have." "You can't expect me to do that; no one does that." "You can't expect me to do this; I don't even know how." On the list goes. That is exactly what the lawyer was doing.

This exposes the big problem in this scenario. Jesus highlighted that the lawyer already knew what to do; he just wasn't doing it. To really grasp this, remember another man who asked some similar questions and also justified himself.

In Luke 18.18-21 a rich young ruler asked the same question as the lawyer's original one: "Good Teacher, what must I do to inherit eternal life?" Jesus listed some laws: "Do not commit adultery, Do not murder, Do not steal, Do not bear false witness, Honor your father and mother." The rich young ruler then tried to justify himself by saying, "All these I have kept from my youth." His conscience was salved by asserting he had kept the Law.

Let's think for a moment. The lawyer could have said the exact same thing in order to justify himself. "I've been doing that, Teacher." But he didn't. He asked a question which in essence explained his excuse for not loving his neighbor. Amazingly enough, the lawyer blamed God—of course, not in so many words. That would have been ridiculous. Even the lawyer knew he wasn't supposed to blame God for his failures to keep the Law. But when you boil it down, the lawyer's follow-up question claimed God simply hadn't been clear enough. As Adam of old blamed "the woman whom you gave to be with me,"[1] this lawyer in essence blamed "the Law which you gave to govern me." He blamed God. It is as if the lawyer was saying, "I want to love my neighbor, really I do. But God hasn't clearly explained who my neighbor is. If you'll explain it, I'll get busy obeying it."

So the lawyer wasn't loving his neighbor, but he felt he could justify himself because he didn't know who his neighbor really

---

[1] Genesis 3.12

was. This is tantamount to the lawyer saying, "I know I'm supposed to love my neighbor, but since I don't know who that is, I'm free and clear. I have a clean conscience. You show me who my neighbor is, and I'll get after loving him. Until then, you can't expect me to do this." That is justifying. He was salving his conscience when he wasn't doing what God said.

And now for the hard mirror question. Do you ever justify yourself? I know I do.

I've known since I was a kid that God's two greatest laws were to love Him and love my neighbor. But how many times have I talked myself out of helping someone in need? How many times have I failed to follow in my Savior's good deed footsteps? How many times do I justify not doing what I know? How many justifications have I come up with to get out of doing what I know is right? Let me share a few.

I Don't Have Enough Information

Like the lawyer I sometimes justify myself by pleading ignorance. "The Bible is just so confusing. It doesn't fully explain this part. I mean, how can I be expected to love my neighbor properly when the lines aren't clearly drawn and I don't know exactly what is right and wrong?" Even after writing four chapters on this parable, I'm still not exactly sure what my limits are. Surely Jesus doesn't expect me to love everyone; that would be impossible. And then questions kick in about various scenarios. The crazy thing is I very often allow scenarios I'm not actually experiencing to keep me from loving my neighbor in the situation I am actually experiencing.

But what we must recognize is Jesus's response to the lawyer demonstrates to us that we know enough. We know we are to love. Do you respond to your neighbor from love? Or from fear, negligence, pride, judgment, haughtiness, convenience, etc.? In any given situation, we don't need to ask a whole bunch of questions about what is technically required of us. We simply need to ask if we loved the person in question.

You Can't Prove I Have To!

As we learned earlier, the lawyer was essentially asking "Who do I have to love?" The corollary is somewhat implied, "What do I have to do to love them?" He wanted a circle drawn around the group he was required to love and around the actions he had to take in order to get eternal life. In other words, "Until you prove to me I have to do this, I'm not going to." There are two problems with this.

First, while God has obviously spelled out that we have to love our neighbor, He has not spelled out a have-to list of deeds and people. That means no one can actually prove you have to do any particular act for any particular person. In other words, I can prove you have to love your neighbor, but if you ask me, "Well, do I have to stop to help a car pulled over on the side of the road?" Or "Do I have to give some money to this person asking me for a handout?" I can't. I can't prove any given particular to you. Of course, keep in mind that also means I can't prove any given particular to other people you wish would love you. Additionally, it doesn't change the fact that if you aren't loving that person, you aren't doing right.

Second, love isn't about have-tos. Think about it like this, wives. If you told your husband, "I really like to receive flowers on my birthday." And he said, "Do I have to get you flowers on your birthday?" You'd probably say something like, "You don't have to, but I really like it." If he didn't give you flowers, would you feel loved? Guys, if you told your wife, "When I get home from work, I really need just 20 minutes of decompression time to unload the stress of the day so I can really connect with you and the kids." If she responded, "Ugh, do I have to do that?" You might say something like, "I guess you don't have to. But it would really help me." When she repeatedly violated that time would you feel loved? Love isn't about "have to." It is about compassion, mercy, and "want to."

What If I Do the Wrong Thing?

If we are already claiming we don't have enough information, we might add this justification. After all, it sounds very noble to cite a fear of doing wrong. We'd hate to do anything wrong. But notice, this does not assert that the thing we are talking about is wrong; we are just talking about the fear of possibly doing something that might be wrong.

I can't help but think about the one talent man of Matthew 25.24-27. He did nothing because he was afraid he would do the wrong thing. Certainly, you may avoid some particular actions because you can't do them in faith. And obviously, this is not permission to do what you know is wrong. But if you are consistently doing nothing to love your neighbors and using this excuse, it is merely self-justification and is not loving.

Someone Might Take Advantage of Me

This is a biggie. Back when I was 22, right before Marita and I got married, I was outside my new apartment unloading furniture I had transported up from Alabama into what was going to be our new home. A man came up and asked for some money. In my mind I was looking at a prospect for the gospel. I had just moved to Dyersburg, Tennessee. It was my first "full-time work" as a gospel preacher. And here I was looking at the first person I was going to baptize. Wouldn't I look great to my new elders and new congregation? I wanted to help and turn that into a Bible study and then a convert. He hit me up a couple of times over the next week. However, the man was a con. When all was said and done, he had swindled me out of $80. That's not such a big deal now, but back then, for me, that was big money. It was more than I made in a day. It was like I had spent a day working, and he got the money for it. After that, you can imagine I became jaded. Nobody was going to take advantage of me again.

Over time, however, I've had to learn, no one goes to hell for being taken advantage of. I'm certainly glad Jesus didn't say to the Father, "I'm not going down there among those ungrateful creatures. What if they take advantage of Me?" I'm not saying be reckless. I am saying love your neighbor and don't justify a lack of love with your fear of being taken advantage of.

I Don't Want to Be a Poor Steward

We might make this justification from two different directions.

First, we might be making a justification similar to our last one. If someone takes our help and uses it to sin, we don't want to be responsible. We obviously don't want to support sinfulness. However, many times the issue is not that we don't help a particular person because we know they will use it to sin. Rather, sometimes we just never help anyone because we are afraid they will sin. If we are trying to help someone from love and they use it to sin, that is on them, not us. If we don't help someone in need, that will be on us because we aren't loving our neighbor.

Second, we might be simply trying to preserve our own

goods. "If I give away too much of what I have, that would be poor stewardship. Where does all this stop?" Chapter 6 deals with healthy boundaries in this area. For now, however, let me explain that, when we use this self-justification, it isn't about healthy boundaries. The problem is the modern prosperity gospels and their baptized cousins (which claim God can do more with Christians who have more) have duped us into misunderstanding what good stewardship actually is.

Go ahead. Answer in your own mind. What does it mean to be a good steward of your finances? Did it sound something like this? Avoid debt. Have an emergency fund. Save for your kids' college and your retirement. Do well financially so you can take care of yourself throughout your old age. And God wants you to do this so you will have plenty left over to help others. But is that really good stewardship?

Let's go back to the rich young ruler who asked Jesus about inheriting eternal life in Luke 18.18. This was the kind of person the world would say is a good steward. In fact, he even seems to be the kind of guy Christian authors and radio hosts would claim was a good steward. But Jesus said he was not a good steward. You see, being a good steward does not mean managing your own goods well. Being a good steward means managing someone else's property well.

But what is the first principle of managing someone else's property? Do what they told you to do with it. Use it the way they told you to use it. The rich young ruler managed his material goods as if they were his own property. While I have no doubt this ruler of the Jews did some good deeds with his riches, his management was designed to make sure his pocket was lined. And he was very successful at that. The problem for him was he wasn't doing what the owner of his property told him to do with it.

Let me ask you this. If you gave me $100 to go pay a bill for you, to put in the collection plate, or to give to another friend, but instead I invested it and made $1000 that I kept for myself before doing what you directed, would that be good stewardship? "But look at all this money I made. I'm a savvy investor." What would you say? Wouldn't you say something like, "But it's my money and I told you what to do with it." Loving our neighbors is great stewardship because it is exactly what God has told us to do with His money.

Please don't misunderstand. I'm not saying having a retirement plan is bad stewardship. I'm simply pointing out that our view of stewardship may be a bit skewed. We cannot claim good stewardship as our excuse to not love our neighbor because the One whose stuff we are stewarding told us to love our neighbors with it.

They Got in This Mess Themselves

This is a subtle form of pride I have used to justify myself way too often. Have you ever done this? From on high, we can look down at others who haven't done as well as we have. Perhaps it is someone who needs consolation because their sin has destroyed their marriage. Perhaps it is someone who needs forgiveness because their sin drove a wedge in our relationship. Perhaps it is someone who needs financial help because they made big financial mistakes, maybe even knowingly.

A great account in Luke 7.36-50 hits me too close to home. A Pharisee invited Jesus over for a meal. While there, a sinful woman (many think that means she was a prostitute) washed Jesus's feet. Simon thought to himself, "Jesus must not be a prophet, otherwise He wouldn't let this woman touch Him." Not only was this unloving, but it was unloving because of pride. Simon was implying he should have been able to touch Jesus because he wasn't as much of a sinner as the woman.

This justification we are talking about results from the same kind of pride. When we refuse to do good to our neighbor because they got themselves into the mess, we are forgetting The Good Deed we started this whole book with. When Jesus looked at us in our mess, He could have said, "They got themselves into this mess. They can get themselves out." But He didn't. Though we were weak, sinful, and ungodly, He paid the price to get us out of our own mess.

Please don't misunderstand. I'm not talking about becoming reckless enablers. However, we must not justify a lack of love by sitting in judgment over those who got themselves into their own messes.

I Don't Even Know This Person

It should seem obvious in the context of the Parable of the Good Samaritan that this statement doesn't justify. After all, the Samaritan didn't know the man. However, let me share an illustration that stuck with me even though the book it came from didn't. Let's say a friend of yours got a job as a waitress. On her first night, you take a group of friends to show your support and give your friend a huge tip. You get there and your friend is just having trouble. The place is packed. She's running around trying to keep up with all her tables. She messes up your order. She doesn't get the drinks out as quickly as you would like. What do you do? Most of us would give the benefit of the doubt to our friend. We know it's her first night. We know everyone has bad nights. We know she isn't purposefully trying to mess up our eating experience. We were there to support her, so we give her the big tip anyway. And we bask in how much we love our neighbor because we know she didn't really deserve that tip, but we gave it out of love for our friend.

But what if it is just a normal night out at a restaurant with a waiter or waitress we don't know, and they do this? Do we chew them out? Do we ask them if everything is all right? Do we report them to the manager? Do we give the benefit of the doubt? Here's someone we don't know. Do we do good deeds to them in this situation, or do we simply take out our frustration because we didn't get the service to which we thought we were entitled?

It's a justification we may subconsciously make. We're not only supposed to love friends but even enemies. How much more should we love strangers who are not at either extreme?

There Is No Justifying Myself

Are there more justifications? I'm sure there are. But these get the point across. If you are like me, we are masters at justifying ourselves just like this lawyer. Here is what I know. The Parable of the Good Samaritan (and many similar passages) are extremely challenging. They don't draw easy lines. They don't allow for simple copouts. And when I read them, my first reaction is often to behave just like the lawyer. I start to justify myself for why I haven't done what it says. Of course, part of the reason for that is because all too often, like the lawyer, I see this as a check-off item I have to accomplish in order to attain eternal life for myself.

If I learn anything from the story of this benevolent Samaritan, it is that if I am going to try to be worthy of eternal life by loving my neighbor, I'm not going to make it. I've already blown it. I have so much growing to do to get to that level of loving everyone all the time that I might as well just give up. None of my justifying can deal with how far I fall short of loving like Jesus Christ. Instead of trying to earn eternal life and trying to justify the places where I haven't, I need to understand I can't earn it. There is no justifying myself.

Jesus Christ died for me, and by faith in Him I will justified. And having been justified, I can allow that justification to change me into the person who is a more like Jesus. I'm not going to gain eternal life by justifying the times I haven't loved. But having been justified by the blood of Jesus Christ I can become a little more like Him this week, passing on to others the love He has given to me a little better.

It will work the same way for you.

5

A Levite, a Priest, and a Samaritan Walk into a Bar

I'd like to tell you a story.

A certain man was traveling from Jerusalem to Jericho when he fell among robbers and thieves. They beat him, stripped him, and left him half dead on the side of the road. By chance a priest was going down that road, and when he saw the man, he passed by on the other side. Likewise a Levite, when he came down that same road and saw the man, he also passed by on the other side. But a Samaritan, as he travelled, came down that very same road. When he saw the man, he had compassion. He went to him and bound up his wounds, treating them with oil and wine. He set the injured man on his own animal and brought him to an inn and took care of him all that night. The next day he took out two days' wages and gave them to the innkeeper, saying, "Take care of him, and whatever more you spend, I will repay you when I come back."

This may seem a bit off the wall, but a friend of mine once asked me, "Hey, do you know how every racist joke starts?" I responded, "No, how?" He started looking over his shoulder and around the room but didn't say anything. It took me a few moments to get it. Sometimes I'm kind of slow on the uptake. But when it struck me what he was doing, I got it. He was demonstrating that ethnic and racist jokes start by the teller looking around to see if anyone of the race or ethnicity that is about to be made fun of is around to hear. Let's face it, racism isn't politically correct anymore (thankfully). That means racism has gone under the cover of darkness for many people. While fewer and fewer people will publically express racism, many are still plagued by the prejudices of it. And this brings up the big elephant in the story of the Good Samaritan.

Depending on how you tell this story, it could almost sound like the beginning of an ethnic joke. How many times have we heard a story that starts something like this: "Hey, a Levite, a Priest, and a Samaritan walk into a bar," or as in our story, "A Levite, a Priest, and a Samaritan walked down a road"? Of course, the problem is this ethnic story doesn't have a punch line. We don't get out of it with a raucous guffaw, a hearty laugh, or even a modest chuckle. We walk away feeling like Jesus has looked deep into our soul and uncovered a dirty little secret.

What makes this story work? Ethnic, racist, religious, and political prejudice. Jesus uncovered a dirty little secret in the lawyer—the man who wouldn't stop a Samaritan from helping him if he was on the road beaten, bleeding, and dying probably wouldn't have helped the Samaritan if roles were reversed.

In a book on the story of the benevolent Samaritan, we cannot overlook this glaring point. We don't love like a Samaritan if we don't love across racial and ethnic lines. When we only love the people who look like us, dress like us, talk like us, and vote like us, then we aren't loving like a Samaritan.

So let's consider some principles to help us take the lesson of loving our neighbor across racial and ethnic lines.

Hurt and Pain Cross Racial Lines

Do you rejoice when your baby is born? So do folks of other races. Do you grieve when someone you love dies? So do folks of other races. Do you get scared for your future when you lose a job? So do folks of other races. Do you bleed when someone cuts you? So do folks of other races. Do you hurt when someone kicks or punches you? So do folks of other races. Do you get upset when someone mocks and ridicules you? So do folks of other races. Do you hunger when you haven't eaten? So do folks of other races. No doubt, there are cultural differences. The way differing cultures express joy, sorrow, pain, etc. may be different. But hurt and pain are universal. You and your kind aren't the only ones who know pain. It didn't matter what race the man lying beaten on the road was. He was in pain. He was afflicted. He needed help. Hurt and pain cross racial lines.

Mercy and Compassion Must Cross Racial Lines

The Samaritan didn't discriminate against the beaten man because of his race. He knew hurt and pain cross the racial line, so his mercy had to cross the racial line.

Jesus Died for All Races

As I read about the Good Samaritan, I can't help but think about how this fits into the context of Jesus's other dealings with Samaritans. In John 4, we read the account of Jesus meeting a Samaritan woman at a well. Though their religion was all messed up, they were looking for the Messiah too. Many of the Samaritans in her village believed on Jesus as the Savior. When we consider John 1.12-13, we recognize those folks were given the right to be children of God. When Jesus died on the cross, He died for Samaritans too. When He died on the cross, he died for blacks, Hispanics, Jews, Indians, Russians, Africans, Mexicans, and, despite all the wicked things we have done, even white Americans. When you see a person of a different race and culture hurting, remember Jesus bore his griefs, carried his sorrows, and went to the cross for him (Isaiah 53.4). What can you do for him?

Don't Believe the Hurting Person
Deserved It Because of His/Her Race

We know Jews and Samaritans despised each other. They no doubt had their own stereotypes for each other. When the Samaritan saw the hurting man on the side of the road, he didn't assume the man deserved it because of his race. He didn't bring up some stereotype that said the man was probably in his mess because Jews were always doing things like this. He didn't assume the man had done this to himself because of his race. You know, it may well be that a person is in a mess because she did something wrong. Haven't we all been there? But here is the key: nobody is in a mess because people of her race are just like that. Since I'm a white guy and usually talk to white people, I can't help but speak about this from a white guy's perspective. Do you realize almost 5 million white people are receiving welfare? Do any of you think that any given white person is receiving welfare because white people are, as a class, lazy freeloaders who don't want to work? Yet, I dare say plenty of white folks have heard about the just over 5 million black people who are receiving welfare and made a general statement about the supposed laziness of the entire race. Get rid of that prejudice.

Don't Let the Worst People in a Race Be
Your Stereotype of That Race

No doubt Jesus broke a mold when He told this story. The reason this story works is because of the racial prejudices and stereotypes the Jewish lawyer would have had against Samaritans. To the lawyer, Samaritans were just bad people. They wouldn't help a man in need. They especially wouldn't help a Jew. And yet, this Samaritan broke the stereotype. But here's the kicker and the subtle racism that we can still have in this situation. We might say, "This Samaritan is different from the rest of them." That is still just as prejudicially racist. "This one is okay. He's more like us. He isn't like the rest of them." We tend to judge our own race by the best of "us" and other races by the worst of "them." Look, I don't care what race we are talking about, there are bad people or people who do bad things in those races. But we must not let the worst people in a race be our stereotype of that race.

I once heard of a black man being asked by a white man for help in overcoming prejudice. The black man said, "Well, I'll admit that some folks in my race don't make it easy." This is just hogwash. Plenty of white people don't make it easy to like whites. Plenty of Hispanics don't make it easy to like Hispanics. Plenty of Indians don't make it easy to like Indians. Just because you can find people in a race who fit your prejudiced stereotype is no justification for having the prejudiced stereotype. The issue is few of us look at our own race through such a stereotypical lens even though we can find people of our own race who do bad things.

In Luke 9.51-56, Jesus and His disciples were headed to Jerusalem and were going through Samaria to get there. He sent messengers to a Samaritan village to make preparations for Him, but the village wouldn't receive Him because He was going to Jerusalem. This village completely measured up to the stereotype most Jews would have had of the Samaritans. But don't forget the Samaritan woman at the well and her village. Don't forget the benevolent Samaritan. I'll repeat: just because you can find people in a race who fit your prejudiced stereotype is no justification for having the prejudiced stereotype.

Quit Thinking Race Defines a Person

Have you ever noticed that Jesus didn't actually tell us what race the beaten man was? I consistently call him a Jewish man because I am certain the lawyer saw him as a Jewish man. That's what we do. When someone tells us a man or a woman did such and such, we see that person in terms most like us. But Jesus didn't actually define the race of the man. Why? Because race doesn't actually define people.

Have you ever told a story and said, "So, I was talking to this blue-eyed guy and he said..."? Or "I was walking out of the store, and I saw a red-headed woman with freckles who did..."? I'm not saying there is never a time when these details matter and should be included in the telling of a story. After all, Jesus did define the man who helped as a Samaritan. Clearly, if you are describing someone you saw leaving the store with stolen merchandise to a police officer and he is looking for an identifying description, you don't say things like, "Well, I don't see skin color." You say, "I saw a red-headed, white woman with freckles." But think about it. I am not defined by the fact that I have freckles. Why would a black man be defined by his skin pigmentation or an Indian be defined by his?

Whenever you tell a story and highlight that the person you are talking about is white, black, Hispanic, Indian, or whatever race, why did you do that? Was it to say, "Don't be surprised by this story I'm about to tell you because the subject is a member of a race that does these things"? Or maybe it was to say, "Be completely shocked; we all know that people of this race don't normally act this way, but this one guy did something completely different." This may not be a 100% rule, but if the pigmentation of a person's hair and eyes is not relevant to the story, you probably don't need to explain the pigmentation of her skin. Race doesn't define people.

Don't Racially Profile Negative Traits and Actions

Have you ever asked yourself who the robbers were in this story? Were they Jews, Samaritans, or Gentiles? Do you think the lawyer had a picture in his mind of what those robbers looked like? Let me ask you this. When you hear about some negative action or trait and you have no idea who actually did it, who do you picture? Do you picture someone in a particular race? If you hear about someone being robbed, do you picture someone of a particular race as the perpetrator? If you were talking to someone about it, would you say, "I bet it was someone of this race. They're always doing that kind of thing"?

How about we just recognize that people of all races do bad things. People of all races do good things. When we hear of a bad action or a good one, why not just let it be a person who did it without having to try to figure out the race? It doesn't make you a good person when you prove the perpetrator of a bad action was from another race. It also doesn't make you a bad person or more likely to do bad things just because someone from your own race did a bad thing.

If You Want to Overcome Discrimination, Serve

Overcoming prejudice is going to take a long time for most of us. We live in a society dominated by prejudices in race, religion, class, politics, education, and region. Overcoming prejudices will take a long time of purposeful restructuring of our thought processes. But the first step to overcoming our prejudices is to overcome our discrimination. Discrimination is acting upon our prejudices. The fact is I don't know what the Samaritan thought of the man in the road. I don't know what prejudices he might have had against the man. But I know he didn't discriminate against the man. Instead, he served him. If we want to overcome discrimination, service is the key. This gets us right back to where we started. The big elephant in the room on this story is that the Samaritan's service, good deeds, and love crossed cultural lines.

Treat people the way you want to be treated, not the way they have or would treat you. Remember that Jesus's answer to the question "Who is my neighbor?" was essentially "Whoever you would want to act like a neighbor if roles were reversed." That brings us to what we call the Golden Rule based on Matthew 7.12: "So whatever you wish that others would do to you, do also to them, for this is the Law and the Prophets."

A Real Life Story

I'd like to tell you about a friend of mine who is now a shepherd in the Lord's church in Beaumont, Texas. His name is Westley. He and I worked together for eight years, and I respect him about as much as anyone else I know.

In 1966, he was a black teenager being bussed to the historically white French High School during forced integration. I asked him about some of these issues and his perspective on how we could help Christians love across racial and ethnic lines. He told me a story he said has guided his interactions with people of every race and background ever since it happened. He said he has made it his goal to never make anyone feel the way he was made to feel in that school.

No one ever asked him if he wanted to go to that school; he just had to go. What was he going to do? As he was bussed in, he was greeted by signs and banners telling him to go back where he came from, telling him he wasn't wanted, telling him he was the problem. Some of those signs were carried by people, some planted in the ground, some taped to the walls. He didn't want to be there any more than the people with those signs wanted him there. But times were changing and someone had to be first. He got to be one of them.

One day, he and some friends were hanging out at the end of their lunch time when a white teacher stepped out of her class room. Immediately she started haranguing them. She used foul language including the "n" word repeatedly. She said all kinds of mean, nasty, and derogatory things, explaining that they were awful troublemakers, needed to go back to Africa (even though every single one of them was as American as she was), and asking why they were such awful people. One of the young men snapped and started to lunge for her. Westley and his friends immediately grabbed the fellow, pulling him back, as he started yelling his own set of obscenities and put-downs to the teacher.

Westley said what happened next shocked him more than anything else in the whole sordid mess. The white woman didn't get in his face and yell even louder. She didn't order him to the principal's office for using foul language. She didn't run away in fear that his friends might let him go and he might attack her. She started crying. She started boo-hooing and blubbering. "How on earth could you say such mean things to me?" she bawled. And it hit Westley. His friend had hurt the woman's feelings. The woman who had just been belittling them and calling them names could sincerely not understand why one of those young men would say those same kinds of things back to her. How could anyone be so blind? And then he got it. This woman thought he was different. She thought he was less human. She had no problem saying to them the very kinds of things that would make her cry, because she didn't see them as people with feelings. She saw them as animals. And that is exactly what Westley felt like as he watched her cry. "She thinks I'm less than human. She thinks I'm an animal." That day he determined he would never make anyone feel the way he was made to feel that day. He committed to treat others the way he wanted to be treated even if they were from a different culture, ethnicity, and race.

And that is the key to love. Few of us would leave a wounded dog on the side of the road, but the Levite and Priest left a wounded man there. The Samaritan didn't see race, ethnicity, or culture. He saw another human being in need of compassion and mercy. So he gave it to him. That day a Samaritan proved to be a better neighbor than a Levite and a Priest. And likely, he proved to be a better neighbor than the lawyer would have been.

If the Parable of the Good Samaritan teaches me anything at all, it is that good deeds and love must cross racial and ethnic lines. There is no room for discrimination with our good deeds. There is no room for prejudice and racism. I must remember that the whole point of this parable is to teach me that the neighbor I must love is anyone I would want to love me if roles were reversed. If I were the one in need, I wouldn't refuse help just because it came from someone of a different race. Why then would I refuse or even just neglect to help that person when roles are reversed?

Jesus was a Middle Eastern Jew when He died for us, right? Let's remember that as we go about doing good.

6

Healthy Boundaries and Proper Priorities

I'd like to tell you a story.

A certain man was traveling from Jerusalem to Jericho when he fell among robbers and thieves. They beat him, stripped him, and left him half dead on the side of the road. By chance a priest was going down that road, and when he saw the man, he passed by on the other side. Likewise a Levite, when he came down that same road and saw the man, he also passed by on the other side. But a Samaritan, as he travelled, came down that very same road. When he saw the man, he had compassion. He went to him and bound up his wounds, treating them with oil and wine. He set the injured man on his own animal and brought him to an inn and took care of him all that night. The next day he took out two days' wages and gave them to the innkeeper, saying, "Take care of him, and whatever more you spend, I will repay you when I come back."

There are no easy answers. The lawyer was clearly hoping to learn some qualifying modifiers to make the command to love his neighbor easier. He was hoping to find a little relief from what seemed like an impossible command. However, Jesus didn't give him any easy outs. He didn't draw any lines. He basically said the lawyer was supposed to prove to be a neighbor to everyone with whom he came in contact. We can hear that profound lesson, be moved by it, but still object, "But I can't do that for everybody. Where does it stop?"

Rarely do we ask the question this way. Rather, the questions I hear (and ask myself) are: "Do I have to stop for every car broken down on the side of the road?" "Do I have to give money to every beggar on the street?" Or I hear (and say): "You can't expect me to visit every sick and shut-in person." "Surely you can't expect me to invite every single person I talk with to have a Bible study." Are there any healthy boundaries or proper priorities?

Remember, Love is a Sacrifice

When the benevolent Samaritan loved his neighbor, he used his own oil and wine. He put the man on his own animal and walked. Have you ever wondered where he got the bandages? He probably wasn't carrying a first aid kit. Rather, he likely ripped up one of his own garments. He used the rest of his day and night to care for the man. Then he gave two days of his wages to the innkeeper and promised to cover any other costs. This one good deed cost the Samaritan. We have to start with this principle: loving our neighbor means sacrifice.

I start here because I fear in my own life I don't really want healthy boundaries on good deeds. I want some plan to do good deeds that doesn't cost me anything. I want to live my life my way to my heart's content and then give up anything I have left over. That is loving me; that is not loving my neighbor.

In Galatians 6.2, Paul talks about loving our brethren and says, "Bear one another's burdens, and so fulfill the law of Christ." What happens when I bear someone else's burdens? I get burdened. If I'm not bearing an extra load, I'm not bearing anybody's burden. It reminds me of the times I've helped people move and see a big piece of furniture. We have six guys picking it up, and I'm running around trying to find a place to grab hold. Finally, I grab it with one hand, but I'm not actually carrying anything. I'm just touching the furniture so it looks like I'm helping. Others are bearing the burden, not me. Too often that is how I want to love my neighbors. I don't want to be burdened.

In the same way, we can do token good deeds to look like we are involved but not really love our neighbors. If there's no sacrifice, no burden, it's not the Good Samaritan's kind of love. And so someone comes forward at the end of the sermon. We hug them and promise to pray for them. But we don't follow up later. In fact, we're a little afraid to because what if they latch on to us and want to talk several times per week? Or how often do we ask if someone needs something because it is the polite thing to do, but if they actually said, "Yes, could you please…" we'd be shocked and a little annoyed. I was called on this one time by an elder (in fact, it was Westley from the prior chapter). He was in the hospital, and I did the polite thing of asking if he needed anything. He responded, "Oh thank you, I need someone to cut my grass." After my look of shock was registered, he let me know his son was taking care of that but was just wondering if I really meant what I offered. He nailed me. Because I didn't really mean it. At least I didn't mean I was willing to do something that would take all afternoon. How often are we willing to love only when it doesn't cost us anything? That's not the kind of love Jesus is talking about.

I start with this point because I hope we all understand that nothing in this chapter is to be taken as an excuse not to love someone in deed and in truth. The goal is to help us have a plan to love in healthy ways, not to justify not loving. For more on that issue, look back to chapter 4 on seeking to justify ourselves.

Prioritizing Our Good Deeds

There is an aspect of impossibility to what we've been talking about. If Jesus says everyone is our neighbor, then we have over 7 billion neighbors in our increasingly global community. Whereas our ancient counterparts often lived and died without venturing out of their 20 mile radius, almost everyone in our part of the world is at least a state traveler, if not a nation traveler or a world traveler. When Jesus told the Parable of the Good Samaritan, if a person didn't actually stumble upon someone in need, he probably would never find out about it. But with the advent of the electronic media, e.g. television news and internet, we know about all kinds of needs. We may not literally cross paths with a homeless man as we travel today, but we know that 15% of Americans are living below the poverty level. On any given night more than 600,000 people in our great nation are homeless and almost half of them are not only homeless but will not have any shelter when they try to sleep tonight. But that is not all. We hear about slave trafficking worldwide. We know abortion needs to be fought and the resulting demand for adoption. We think of the billions of lost people who need the gospel. We hear about Christians who are struggling emotionally, spiritually, financially, and on the list goes. No wonder we see a person asking for help and feel an overwhelming burden and sense of guilt.

We must not do nothing just because we can't do everything. One biblical principle helps me: "For if the readiness is there, it is acceptable according to what a person has, not according to what he does not have."[1] Let's face it, we can't do everything. That is impossible. And praise the Lord, that isn't the requirement. We all only have 24 hours/day. We each have our own amount of resources, some more, some less. We just can't do it all. We can't respond to every need expressed in our global society. While God doesn't expect from us what we don't have, He does expect what we do have. And as we said, He does expect us to sacrifice. Even the Macedonians had done according to 2 Corinthians 8.3-4: "For they gave according to their means, as I can testify, and beyond their means, of their own accord, begging us earnestly for the favor of taking part in the relief of the saints…"

On a practical level, this reminds me of what John Maxwell tells us about our time. We all have enough time to do anything we want, but we don't have enough time to do everything we want. That means we must prioritize. In the financial realm we may not have enough money to do anything we want, which highlights the point even more. When it comes to good deeds, we have to prioritize. What is a healthy way to do that? The Bible actually provides some great principles of prioritization.

Priority #1: Family

1 Timothy 5.8 explains that anyone who doesn't provide for his relatives, especially his own household, is worse than an unbeliever. Our family takes a priority for us. In other words, taking necessary food, clothing, and shelter from our kids to give to someone else is not being a good steward of God's blessings. Now, that's not the same as withholding good deeds from our neighbor because we want to first make sure our kids get to be involved in every extracurricular activity their heart desires,

---

[1] 2 Corinthians 8.12

have every gizmo and gadget they want, and have a closet full of designer clothes. But we do see that family takes a priority.

Priority #2: Spiritual Family

Galatians 6.10 says, "So then, as we have opportunity, let us do good to everyone, and especially to those who are of the household of faith." This passage explains that, while we should do good deeds for anyone, our brethren should take precedence. Notice, this doesn't say we only do good deeds for Christians, but it does say we especially make sure to do good for our brothers and sisters. If we have brethren in the congregation going without but we consistently send our aid to folks in the world, we are simply not being good stewards of God's blessings to us. I know we long to make this about evangelism. But God has never presented our good deeds as the means of evangelism. I would long for all of us to remember that God has asked us all to seek first His kingdom and righteousness and then He'll add to us the material needs we pursue.[2] We must not make the bedrock of our evangelism the reverse of this principle, trying to give to the world all those other needs so that hopefully they'll pursue God's kingdom and righteousness.

Priority #3: Our Community

Some stipulations in the Old Covenant can give us some insight to a next level of priority. Multiple passages show this, but I'll just select one. Deuteronomy 14.28-29 addresses the tithe. It was to be used to help the Levites, the widows, the orphans, and the sojourners in the town. The "sojourner" was a non-Jew who lived in the town with the Jews. We get a good principle from this to help us out. Our own community should take some

---

[2] Matthew 6.33

precedence in our good deeds. Are we really loving our neighbor if we make an annual contribution to the "Hungry Children's Fund of South Africa" but we aren't helping any of the needy and hungry children in our home towns or home states? I guarantee you there are needy folks nearby.

Again, please don't use this as some excuse not to help in some case of urgent need you learn about just because it doesn't fit neatly into your priority plan (cf. Titus 3.14). At the same time, don't beat yourself up because you can't do everything. Prioritize.

Let Love Limit Love

The next question is how far should we take this? Should I give something to every person begging for aid? Should I keep giving to someone who misuses what I give him? The answer to that question is not easy. If you're like me, you want a line drawn. "Give this much, no more." "Give to these people, not those people." "Give this many times and your love is fulfilled." It doesn't work like that.

The answer to this question is found in the command itself. "You shall love...your neighbor as yourself." The passage does not say I have to give money to everyone who asks. But I do have to love everyone with whom I come in contact. Therefore, the question in any given situation is not "Did I give someone money?" The question is "Did I love them?" This brings us to the healthy boundary: let love limit love.[3]

So let's get this down to brass tacks. Let's use an extreme case to illustrate. You're walking downtown and you pass a guy

---

[3] I wish I had come up with that little power statement on my own, but I didn't. Though it is indicated by the command itself, this statement comes from *Ministries of Mercy: The Call of the Jericho Road* by Tim Keller.

with a sign that says, "Homeless vet. I'm hungry…please give." Are you aware that just because someone gives the man money doesn't mean they love him, and just because someone doesn't give him money doesn't mean they don't love him? Many who give to the man aren't responding to this man in love. Rather, some are responding from guilt: "I read that book on loving my neighbor; guess I have to give." Some are responding from shame: "I feel so bad because I have so many blessings this guy doesn't have. I'm just part of that evil capitalist culture. I should give." Others are responding from convenience: "I know that loving someone means getting to know them and trying to really help them, but I don't have time for that. It is so much easier just to drop a buck in his can." In each case, these people give the man money, but they don't love their neighbor.

We also need to understand that loving is not the same as enabling. When we have good reason to believe a person is just being enabled to pursue sin or folly by a financial donation, we are not loving that person by giving them money. In that case, we are actually hurting them. However, that doesn't mean the loving thing is to do nothing. Neither is the loving thing to drop a note in his can that says, "Get a job!" It's not convenient, but instead of just walking by and either handing out five bucks or looking the other way awkwardly, why not invite the guy into the nearest restaurant? Buy him lunch and then start getting to know him? Why not ask him if he likes where his life is? Why not ask him if he would like to escape that situation? Let him know you're a child of God who longs to help people, but that means so much more than giving a handout or a free meal. Let him know you want to be of help to him, but that means being invited into his whole life, not just his lunch time. If he's interested, you may have met someone you can really love. If he says, "No, thanks," then you know the loving thing to do is not enable the man to live this way by continuing to give handouts.

Maybe you really don't have time in the moment you meet this man for this lengthy exchange. Perhaps you can come up with a shorter version like Peter and John did in Acts 3.6: "I don't have any money for you. But I'll tell you what I do have. I have a lot of love, and I'd like to spend some time with you, helping you get on your feet. I can't talk much now, but if there's a time we can get together and talk about how Jesus helped me and how He can help you too, when would that be and where could we meet?"

This is one extreme situation that I hope illustrated the point. Do you have to give money to every beggar you see? No, of course not. But you do have to love every beggar, every person you see. That is the question. Was your response to them love or something else?

Seven Kinds of Good

This point could and probably should be an entire book all on its own. But another problem we often have is just looking at all the different kinds of good works that are out there. We actually do pursue some good works, but then we hear a lesson about a particular kind of good work that we don't do much of, and we start beating ourselves up as bad Christians who don't love our neighbors. This is neither fair nor right. Again, I don't want to provide wiggle room for avoiding good works. However, there is a good biblical principle that should provide us comfort here.

In Romans 12.6-8, Paul presents seven kinds of good. The seven different "kinds" of Christians are servants, teachers, exhorters, sharers, leaders, givers of mercy, and discerners (my more mundane name for the non-miraculous qualities that go along with the "gift of prophecy" mentioned in this passage). The fact is teachers and exhorters are much more likely to conduct Bible studies, pursue what we commonly call personal evangelism, and preach sermons. Givers of mercy and servants are much more likely to shovel a widow's driveway, visit the shut-in in a nursing home, provide a meal for a hungry person. Discerners and leaders are much more likely to confront someone caught up in sin or counsel someone to help them overcome whatever has brought them to need a handout. Sharers are much more likely to give a handout. These people are wired in different ways and are therefore more likely to notice and pick up on different good works.

Don't misunderstand. Titus 3.14 insists we must be devoted to good works, helping in cases of urgent need. You may be a teacher and doing all kinds of good works in teaching. If you see an urgent emotional need in someone, for instance someone crying over the loss of a loved one or a failed marriage, you can't say, "That's not my gift. Too bad for you." You may be a servant and doing all kinds of wonderful acts of service. If you see an urgent teaching need in someone, for instance a lost friend asking you a Bible question, you can't say, "That's not my gift. Too bad for you." Neither of these examples is loving. However, we all need to understand there are different kinds of good works. Everyone will naturally gravitate to the ones that fit their gifts, and we shouldn't sit in judgment just because someone else isn't involved in our good works or heap guilt on ourselves because we aren't involved in all the good works others are doing.

Having said all of that, this is not a free pass on good works. Let's not play games like we have no gifts so we don't have to do good works. If you want to justify not doing much serving because you're more of a teacher, then what good works are you doing in your family, in your congregation, and in your community when it comes to teaching? If you want to justify not doing much in the way of spreading the gospel through teaching because you are more of a servant, then what good works are you doing in your family, in your congregation, and in your community when it comes to serving?

The Final Question

So here is the final question on these boundaries and priorities. Can you pinpoint the sacrifices you are making? What are your good deeds costing you? Do you see a time sacrifice? A financial burden? An emotional, psychological, or spiritual burden? We can set healthy priorities, establish healthy boundaries that are love, and even highlight what kind of good deeds we are going to naturally gravitate to. But if we can't show the sacrifice, we can't claim to love as the Good Samaritan did. That kind of love costs. That kind of love sacrifices. That kind of love bears burdens. But that is the kind of love Jesus has for us. How are you doing at that?

7

LET THE CHURCH NOT BE BURDENED

I'd like to tell you a story.

A Jewish man was going down from Jerusalem to Jericho, and he fell among robbers, who stripped him and beat him and departed, leaving him half dead. By chance, a priest was going down that road. When the priest saw the beaten man, he passed by on the other side of the road. Sometime later, a Levite was also walking down that road. When he saw the beaten man, he also passed by on the other side. Sometime later, a Samaritan, a man hated by Jews, came to the place where the man was. The Samaritan, having compassion on the man said to him, "You are so lucky that I'm part of the Good Samaritan Society. We have funds and resources to deal with this very thing." He called up the nearest outreach manager of the Good Samaritan Society and had him come meet the man. Together they bandaged him up, put him in the Good Samaritan Society's chariot, and gave him a ride to the nearest Good Samaritan Society medical facility, where the Samaritan left the man in the good hands of the organization to which he had given so much money in the past.

Okay, I know you skipped the story. You've already read it seven times and thought you'd save a little time by skipping it here in the final chapter. Don't. Go back and read it. It's different this time. I promise.

Okay, good you read it. I hope by this time you've read the story of the Good Samaritan enough to recognize where this version went astray. And yet the way the modern religious world and mainstream denominationalism conducts good works, you would almost think that is exactly what this story says. In fact, the idea that the local congregation is supposed to be an organization that institutionalizes all potential good works and whose main function is to uphold social justice is all but unquestioned in "American Christianity." Some churches pursue this as a means of outreach and sharing the gospel with the lost. Others simply pursue it because they believe the church's job is to change society itself to be more godly. It is almost like they don't see the world as the enemy of the church but as the great project of the church. Getting into the theology of this Social Gospel is beyond the scope of this book. However, I'd like to get down to some brass tacks about the local church's place in loving our neighbors and being zealous for good deeds. I'd like to look at an often overlooked passage tucked into 1 Timothy 5.16: "If any believing woman has relatives who are widows, let her care for them. Let the church not be burdened, so that it may care for those who are truly widows." While we'll cover a couple of concepts, I'd like to make sure we recognize one main thing. As individual Christians, we are responsible to unburden the local church. This is not so much a regulation for congregational work as it is an explanation of individual responsibility.

While the Church Is Always the People,
the People Are Not Always Acting as the Church

When you think "church," what do you think? Do you think of a building? ("My church is on Fill-In-The-Blank Road.") Do you think of a service? ("We have church at 10:30 on Sundays.") While I understand there is a sense in which these are both true statements based on how the English word is defined and modern usage, neither one of these ideas accurately represents what the New Testament means when it uses the word "church."

In the New Testament, the word "church" is synonymous with our English word "assembly." When you think of an assembly, what do you think of? An assembly is a gathering of people. That is what a church is. It is a gathering of people. Therefore, when you think of a local church, you shouldn't think of the building where the church meets or even the time when the church meets. You should think of the people that meet. In the New Testament, the church is always the people.

However, 1 Timothy 5.16 makes a profound point. While the church is always the people, the people are not always acting as the church. Just because the members of a congregation are doing something doesn't mean the church is doing it. Paul said an individual believer should take care of her dependent widows so the congregation would not be burdened with that work. Here, an individual member is doing the work. If an individual doing work is the same as the congregation doing the work, it would be impossible for the church not to be burdened when the individual is doing the work.

If a Christian lies or commits fornication, would we say the church lied or committed fornication? Of course not. Why then when a Christian feeds a homeless person would we say that the church is feeding homeless people? We understand this with other institutions. If a member of Toastmasters gives a speech at her corporation's conference, did Toastmasters give the speech? A Boy Scout may help a little old lady across the road, but that is not the Boy Scouts helping a little old lady across the road. Similarly, just because a member of your family does something, that doesn't mean the family did it. The same is true with the congregation. There is a difference between individual action and congregational action.

Christians Have Responsibilities that the Local Church Does Not

It is important to distinguish between what we as individuals are supposed to do and are allowed to do and what the local congregation is supposed to do and is allowed to do.

Are there qualifications placed on the widows that individual Christians are to support? No. The text simply says if a Christian won't take care of his/her family members, he/she is worse than an unbeliever.[1] The widow doesn't have to be a Christian; she's just a dependent widow. But notice that the congregation definitely has qualifications and stipulations. She must be at least 60 years old, the wife of one husband (a one-man woman), a woman with a reputation of good works, a Christian who has set her hope fully on God, and one who is not self-indulgent.[2]

In other words, you as an individual Christian have responsibilities that the church doesn't have. Whether or not your widowed mother or grandmother is a faithful Christian, you are worse than an infidel if you won't support her in her need. However, if a widow is not a faithful Christian, the local con-

---

[1] 1 Timothy 5.8
[2] 1 Timothy 5.9-14

gregation is not authorized to support her. That is not because churches don't love widows or don't care about widows who aren't Christians. It is simply because God has a plan for His church.

The Local Church Must Stay Focused on Its Purpose

1 Timothy 5.16 explains more about this distinction between the individual and the local congregation. Regrettably, it is an explanation increasingly lost on people today and even on Christians today. Paul says the reason individuals are to do their good work of supporting their dependent widows (and actually their family) is so the church will not be burdened. That is, so it will not be hindered from functioning properly and accomplishing its true purpose.

Please understand what this means. For too long, Christians and gospel preaching churches have been arguing simply over a rule and a regulation. Churches and Christians on all sides have made this debate about who is keeping a rule better and have all but forgotten what the issue behind all of this is. The point is not for us to figure out a rule and then prove we are following it better. The point is that God has a purpose for the local congregation, and we as individuals are to keep the church unburdened so it can do the work God has given it.

What work has God given the church? We can find three works demonstrated by 1 Timothy and supported in the rest of the New Testament.

Work #1: Proclaim the Truth. According to 1 Timothy 3.15, the church is a "pillar and buttress of the truth." According to 1 Timothy 2.4, folks are saved by knowledge of the truth. Remember John 8.32-36 explains that the truth sets people free from sin. And in John 17.17, we understand that God's truth sanctifies people. The local church's job is to uphold that truth, to lift it up for all the world to see, to expound it so even those in the church can grow.

Work #2: Glorify God. 1 Timothy begins and ends with a profession of the glory of God. 1 Timothy 1.17 says, "To the King of ages, immortal, invisible, the only God, be honor and glory forever and ever. Amen." And 1 Timothy 6.15-16 declares, "…he who is the blessed and only Sovereign, the King of kings and the Lord of lords, who alone has immortality, who dwells in unapproachable light, whom no one has ever seen or can see. To him be honor and eternal dominion. Amen." As Ephesians 3.21 says about God, "to him be glory in the church and in Christ Jesus throughout all generations, forever and ever. Amen." The local church is responsible to bring glory to God, honoring and praising Him.

Work #3: Care for the Family. In 1 Timothy 5.16, Paul specifically says that individual Christians should take care of their own dependent widows so the church will not be hindered from caring for those who are truly widows or widows indeed. But notice the first qualification for those widows is that they are faithful Christians who have set their hope fully on God.[3] These are widows who are in the family of God. Remember, the church is God's household and family.[4] If the household of God doesn't take care of its dependent family members, are we not also worse than unbelievers? But if the local congregation gets burdened, as so many today lead us to believe that the local church is supposed to care for the entire world, how will it fulfill its own mission?

---

[3] 1 Timothy 5.5
[4] 1 Timothy 3.15

In almost every other organization in the world, we recognize how important this principle is. Consider Alcoholics Anonymous. Listen to their fifth and sixth traditions: "5. Each group has but one primary purpose—to carry its message to the alcoholic that still suffers. 6. An A.A. group ought never endorse, finance, or lend the A.A. name to any related facility or outside enterprise, lest problems of money, property, and prestige divert us from our primary purpose."[5] If you called up Alcoholics Anonymous and asked them to donate some money to the American Cancer Society, an orphan's home, or to provide for widows, they would say "No" because that would hinder and divert them from their primary purpose. However, do you believe any member of Alcoholics Anonymous ever gives to the American Cancer Society or takes care of orphans and widows? Of course some do. Do you think any Alcoholics Anonymous group runs an inner city coat closet for the homeless? No. That would divert them from their purpose. However, do you think any member of Alcoholics Anonymous donates, works at, or even runs an inner city coat closet? I can almost guarantee you some do, since many recovering alcoholics have been homeless and long to help their fellow sufferers in this kind of way. Now, do you think Alcoholics Anonymous hates people with cancer, poor people, the homeless, orphans, widows, etc.? Do you think anyone ever even accuses that institution of hating these people? Of course not. Does Alcoholics Anonymous think that running orphan's homes, hospitals, nursing homes, inner city coat closets, etc. are bad works? Of course not. Would anyone accuse them of such? No way. We all know they would believe these are all good works, they just aren't the good works Alcoholics Anonymous was set up to accomplish.

---

[5] http://www.aa.org/en_pdfs/smf-122_en.pdf

We all recognize the necessity for an organization to maintain its focus on its primary purpose without becoming distracted even by other decent and good causes. Why do we have such a hard time understanding that with the local congregation? Sadly, this has happened because too many churches have allowed the world to set their agenda and purpose rather than God.

Christians Must Keep the Local Church Unburdened

Now here's the clincher for us. If you've gotten bored by some of the technical discussion up to this point, wake up. Pay attention to this point. 1 Timothy 5.16 is an instruction to individuals, not to local churches. That is, Paul wasn't telling local churches to make sure they didn't get burdened; he was telling individual Christians to fulfill their responsibility of doing good deeds so the local church would not get burdened with them.

Isn't that exactly what has happened in our modern world? Christians haven't been taking up the mantle of loving their neighbor, so churches have developed programs that divert time, finances, and resources from the primary purpose of the local church. Sadly, many today have determined that the work of the church is to save society rather than to save sinners. We need to remember the difference. We need to remember which is the church's work and which isn't. Jesus didn't come to restore social order. He didn't come to redeem governments and nations. He came to seek and save the lost (Luke 19.10). The church, His body must carry on His mission without being diverted, burdened, or hindered.

Hopefully, we have learned from this book that a person who has been saved by the love of Jesus Christ will no doubt become a person who loves his/her neighbor. That love will be demonstrated in many ways. But the local church is to funnel that love into a focus on glorifying God and setting people free from their sins. And we as individuals are to fulfill our responsibilities so the church will not be burdened by them and be hindered from accomplishing its work.

No doubt, as with every individual responsibility placed on us by the gospel of Jesus Christ, the local church is to teach us, train us, and equip us to go out and love our neighbors in every way possible. The local church may even make us aware of opportunities. Many of us may even band together to do the good works and help in cases of urgent need. We may band together because we have this relationship in this local congregation. However, we must make sure that we keep the local church unburdened from our responsibilities so the congregation won't be hindered and diverted from its God-glorifying, truth-proclaiming, family-caring mission.

We are to be Good Samaritans instead of turning the local congregation into The Good Samaritan Society.

EPILOGUE

I'd like to end with a story.

A certain man was traveling from Jerusalem to Jericho when he fell among robbers and thieves. They beat him, stripped him, and left him half dead on the side of the road. By chance a priest was going down that road, and when he saw the man, he passed by on the other side. Likewise a Levite, when he came down that same road and saw the man, he also passed by on the other side. But a Samaritan, as he travelled, came down that very same road. When he saw the man, he had compassion. He went to him and bound up his wounds, treating them with oil and wine. He set the injured man on his own animal and brought him to an inn and took care of him all that night. The next day he took out two days' wages and gave them to the innkeeper, saying, "Take care of him, and whatever more you spend, I will repay you when I come back."

What a powerfully challenging story it is. I need to be reminded of it again and again and again. Like watchfulness in prayer, I too often have to admit my spirit is willing but my flesh is weak. It is just too easy to get caught up in daily concerns. I can be in such a hurry to move on to my next task that I miss the people around me who need to be loved.

I am so glad Jesus proved to be a good neighbor to me. I'm glad He proved to be one for you also. May we take His love and let it grow us into better neighbors, not off in the distant future but today.

www.ingramcontent.com/pod-product-compliance
Lightning Source LLC
Chambersburg PA
CBHW031630040426
42452CB00007B/767